WHEREAS

WHEREAS

poems

STEPHEN
DUNN

W. W. NORTON & COMPANY

INDEPENDENT PUBLISHERS SINCE 1923

NEW YORK · LONDON

For information about permission to reproduce selections from this book,
write to Permissions, W. W. Norton & Company, Inc.,
500 Fifth Avenue, New York, NY 10110

For information about special discounts for bulk purchases, please contact
W. W. Norton Special Sales at specialsales@wwnorton.com or 800-233-4830

Manufacturing by RR Donnelley
Production manager: Lauren Abbate

ISBN: 978-0-393-25467-9

W. W. Norton & Company, Inc.
500 Fifth Avenue, New York, N.Y. 10110
www.wwnorton.com

W. W. Norton & Company Ltd.
15 Carlisle Street, London W1D 3BS

1 2 3 4 5 6 7 8 9 0

For Madeleine Deininger

CONTENTS

ACKNOWLEDGMENTS

The following poems were published or are about to be published in these journals:

APR: "A Card from Me to Me," "If it's True," "Nothing Personal," "The First Person"
Catch Up: "Why We Need Unions"
The Georgia Review: "Men Falling," "In the Land of Superstition," "Let's Say"
The Journal of American Poetry: "Call Them All In"
New Letters: "For Some a Mountain," "The Invisible Man Blues"
New England Review: "At the School for the Deaf"
New Ohio Review: "An Evolution of Prayer"
The New Yorker: "Ambush at Five O'Clock," "Whereas the Animal I Cannot Help But Be," "Unnatural," "Emergings"
The Paris Review: "Creatures," "The Famous Man," "In Other Words," "The Melancholy of the Nude," "The Owner of the Boutique at Redwood Falls"
Ploughshares: "The Architect"
Plume: "A Short History of Long Ago," "Moon Song"
Poetry: "Always Something More Beautiful," "Propositions"
The Southern Review: "Even the Awful," "The Revolt of the Turtles" (chosen for a 2016 Pushcart Prize)
"Impediment" appeared in *Edward Hopper*, edited by Gail Levin (Crown Publishers)

Thanks to my faithful and critical readers Lawrence Raab, Barbara Hurd, Philip Dacey, Jill Rosser, Sam Toperoff, and for residencies at Yaddo and MacDowell.

A CARD FROM ME TO ME

The pilgrimage of the body from infancy to dust to nothingness,
and the oasis, some believe, of a heaven afterward, every nationality
on their knees, sipping, taking turns, even the reverent sharing with folks
like me. At the very least cake and candle celebrations along the way,
a few people happy for your next *next*, others not as jealous
as they might be, the movement (if we're lucky) from ignorance
to astonishment, allowing for a thousand dumb days in between.
And seeds becoming tomatoes and redwoods, ants becoming armies,
language allowing us to disguise what we mean, *sky* one syllable
for all that complexity, and starfish making their homes in the sea.
I praise on my seventy-fifth birthday the strangeness, the immensity, of what I have
and have had and every small thing that against the odds continues to be.

I

PROPOSITIONS

What does a pig know about bacon?
—Randall Jarrell

Anyone who begins a sentence with, "In all honesty…"
is about to tell a lie. Anyone who says, "This is how I feel"
had better love form more than disclosure. Same for anyone
who thinks he thinks well because he had a thought.

If you say, "You're ugly" to an ugly person—no credit
for honesty, which must always be a discovery, an act
that qualifies as an achievement. If you persist
you're just a cruel bastard, a pig without a mirror,

somebody who hasn't examined himself enough.
A hesitation hints at an attempt to be honest, suggests
a difficulty is present. A good sentence needs
a clause or two, interruptions, set off by commas,

evidence of a slowing down, a rethinking.
Before I asked my wife to marry me, I told her
I'd never be fully honest. No one, she said,
had ever said that to her. I was trying

to be radically honest, I said, but in fact
had another motive. A claim without a "but" in it
is, at best, only half true. In all honesty,
I was asking in advance to be forgiven.

1

CREATURES

The dolphin was all undulation,
riding its whims and churning
the ocean, dorsal fin and bottlenose
alternately visible. A pelican followed it,
not interested, as I wasn't either,
in the splendor of the occasion.
The pelican was soon full
of what could have been a school
of anchovy or mullet, a school where
some could escape the acceptable cruelty
of nature, others put in that halfway house
between maw and digestion.
From the shore where I stood, my dog
barked at what he must
have seen as good animal fun,
or once again a creature
with a big mouth having its way.
I took it all in, thinking that to step out
of our houses any morning is to risk
being variously selected, and that nothing
like kindness or beauty or justice
will ever change the truth of some lives.

MOON SONG

The moon's silence was an invitation to invent its powers,
so when in love we spoke about its influence,
how, even when it was on the other side
of the world, we felt it urging us toward each other.
We'd known for years it could move oceans, cause catastrophes,
but these days it seemed more powerful than ever—

levees broken, towns under water, heartrending diminutions.
It happened with and without us, was never our fault.
Once we might have blamed a vengeful god,
long since forsaken. Now we looked to meteorologists
for explanations, and with visible excitement

they gave us what we needed, those daily portals into havoc,
which allowed us to be elsewhere, on a couch, say,
in a distant living room with an alibi, as if someone else
were responsible. Nighttime or daytime, the moon rewired
our universe. Words came to us, and we turned
them into song. We even learned to believe them.

You need to let rise into daylight
what you've seen on the darkest of nights,
as well as those trivial sepia silhouettes
of bodies moving in nearby apartments.
No matter who you are, a little variety never hurts.

It's possible to rethink that reddish full moon
coming toward you across the bay,
to change even the feel of it as it approaches.
That is, if you want to be true to life,
not entirely to the one you live.

Don't hesitate to include the pink Cadillac
that may or may not have driven by
while you were eating macaroni and cheese,
or those meteors that fell at sensational speeds,
dissolving into nothingness.

You need to remember it's likely
something nameless is governing you,
which is perhaps why your dreams
often turn odd and grave: you're lost at sea
and the sharks are pretending to be dolphins:

In another you're your own secret agent,
gathering evidence, never quite sure
if by mistake you'll turn yourself in. A man
like you is always in danger of getting things
wrong. No rapturous solutions in the offing.

What you need to understand is the mystery
every family harbors. Dig deeper and deeper still.
Under the photos will likely be that packet of letters
tied with a black ribbon, and the sudden uprush
of what you didn't, couldn't, until now ever know.

If it's true that objects retain their memories
of being handled, used, even properly admired
for their efficiency, like a spoon, or diminished,
like a toothpick that once was part of something
grand, like a pine or a sequoia,

      then it's no wonder that some objects
carry themselves with a kind of stainless dignity,
while others seem to enjoy revenge, become splinters
under our fingernails, never forget their capacity
      to right a misuse.

      And if it's true that all objects
made by us soon take on their own personalities,
yet also are driven by what we can't conceal in ourselves,
this may account for the kind of Frankensteinian power—
meltdowns, monstrous behavior—our children,

no matter how loved, develop to withstand our willfulness.
And if it's true that they remember being treated
like cogs or toothpicks, or even machines that work perfectly
in public, let us not be surprised when, years later,
      they break down in private.

CALL THEM ALL IN

> *From the place where we are right*
> *flowers will never grow.*
> —Yehuda Amichai, tr. by Chana Bloch
> and Stephen Mitchell

Call in a Socrates from the streets
to probe and test and resist

so we might learn what's keepable
by knowing what can't be kept.

Call him in, the smart bastard.
I'm sure there must be minds
open enough to be lit anew,

yet I'm thinking there must be others
who might worry almost intelligently

that things *can* grow
out of certain certainties. Call in
a sophist then, someone like myself,

who'd maintain for as long
as he could that he was right too.
Some truths *are* better than others,

which means, of course, some are worse.
Seems time to call in from the vast nowhere
some great adjudicator, some poet

who will arrive to hear both sides.
I have no agenda, he lies,

and proceeds to ask,
How many dead flowers
is anyone's certainty worth to him?

I've already closed my mind,
and, before he goes on, I say I'd sacrifice
not one flower but an entire garden

for what I think I know— a statement
outrageous, gut-driven, pure sophistry,
without proof, beyond proving.

It's where black cats tend to live longer
than their allotted nines, and we avoid
cracks in the sidewalk to ward off whatever
might happen in the whatever places
of our minds. And on certain Fridays
when the thirteenth comes around,
we're comforted that large hotels share
our concerns, allow us to skip entire floors.
It's a safe place for those who toss salt
over their shoulders, or for that man
we've seen bending down to scold flowers
for no apparent reason. When we're like him,
or in love, on the verge of being lost,
which one of us doesn't need some kind
of magic to help navigate and go on?
We dig up a footprint of hers and put it
in a flowerpot. Then plant a marigold,
the flower that takes a while to fade.
Sometimes it works. If not, we find out fast
if all along she was planning to leave.
The superstitious can't help but play
the roulette of this or that, yet understand
those who decry the miraculous. We just
don't desire their world. We build bonfires
and dance beyond midnight to usher in
the much-needed rain. If nothing happens,
we keep dancing in the fiery dark,
all the while inventing great stories

with heroes and heroines. In this way
we create the world we want to live in,
wild, luminescent, a perpetual fiesta
with secret rules and a guest list made up
of people yet to earn their names.

AN EVOLUTION OF PRAYER

As a child, some of his prayers were answered
because he prayed out loud for a kite or bike,
which his mother would overhear, and pass on
to her husband, his father, the Lord.

Later, he understood that when he prayed
he was mostly talking to himself—albeit a better,
more moral part of himself—which accounted
for why he heard nothing back from the void.

Lord, he'd begin, because he was afraid
to alter the language of prayer, Lord, deliver
me from envy and mean-spiritedness,
allow me to love people as I love animals.

Then his father died, and he became the sad Lord
of himself, praying for pleasures immediate and grantable.
Let me tango the night long with Margot the receptionist,
he'd say to no one. Let me do unto others.

THE INVISIBLE MAN BLUES

If I were invisible, I might want to inhabit
the privacies of certain rooms, hang around
before the bank closed, linger in a shower stall
until you disrobed. I could easily leave
any scene unseen. But where to go? And would
you dare join me, become my conspicuous one?

I'd be the slippery criminal, you the accomplice
they'd catch with the goods. A song might begin,
sad, unmelodious, ours. It would say how unfair
the world could be to those who couldn't hide.
It would say how lonely things can be
for those who can't be seen. I'd no doubt start

to see the invisible everywhere—
walking the streets, sitting with others at meetings
and meals, spoken through, around, not to.
The song takes on grit, hurts the both of us,
but with luck I think I'll forever hear it,
evidence of a privilege I'd no longer want.

UNNATURAL

I'm sure Nature has disapproved of me
for years, as if it had overheard
one of my silent screeds against it,
and my insistence that only the artificial
has a real shot at becoming more
than what we started with, designed,
revised, something completely itself.
If it could speak, Nature might say
it contains lilies, the strange beauty
of swamps, the architectural art
of spiders, the many etceteras
that make the world the world.
Nothing man-made can compete,
Nature might say. Oh Nature
has been known to go on and on.
And if it wanted to push things further,
it could site our sleek perfection
of bombs and instruments of torture,
our nature so human we hide
behind words that disguise and justify.
But that's as generous as I want to be
in giving Nature its say. I've seen it
randomly play its violence card—
natural, no-motive crimes
with hail and rain and vicious winds
taking out, say, trailer courts and
playing fields and homes for the elderly.
So I want to be heard and overheard,

this time for real, out loud, in fact
right in Nature's face, to say I prefer
the artifice in what's called artificial,
the often concealed skill involved,
without which we'd have no accurate
view of ourselves, or of lilies in a pond.

Let's say men and women begin
as slime, and some of us crawl
out of the sea, and fall into circumstance
fraught with danger and cannot survive,
but do, slithering into a cave
where the stories evolve, first as pictures
on the walls, then as grunts that turn
into something like words. For years,
though, biology reigns. Our bodies go
this way or that. Our culinary wisdom
is to eat more then get eaten.
Our good sense is to follow a guess.
Let's say sometimes the accidental
is the beginning of possibility.
We discover that when most afraid,
when catastrophe looms, opportunities abound.
We learn the power of slings and stones.
And the best storyteller emerges
from all of those wishing to explain.
Let's say he knows we need someone
to admire, and says a hero is a person
who blunders into an open cave
and that it takes courage to blunder.
Let's say he also says something about
the beauty of slime. His story lives
for a while because of its memorable turns,
its strange moral fervor, while the others'—
merely accurate and true—disappear.

II

WHEREAS THE ANIMAL I CANNOT HELP BUT BE

The possum knows how to play himself,
is one of us. And the chameleon,
too, can fit right in, be other than it is.
I praise them both.

And as night rises up from the grass
and comes down from the clouds,
bats at top speed merely glance
off of what they disturb.

I admire their swooping gracefulness,
and the brilliance of moles carving tunnels
under lawns, feeling their whiskery way
as they go. I even praise the cat,

its savage patience and quick paws.
And feel a camaraderie with the earthworm,
straightforward but slippery, both ends open,
getting under the feet of barefoot girls.

Unlike you and me, they have no choice.
They themselves are evidence
of what can be done conspicuously,
or undercover, without remorse.

Whereas the animal I cannot help but be,
duplicitous, having more than once been taken
to task, shamed, still envies the silver fox,
leaving a false trail, swerving this way, then that.

First, out of the scraps of dreams,
and later out of the clashing loyalties
of belief and skepticism,
he believed he could live
a thoughtful, occasionally principled life.
If he couldn't be a man for all seasons,
certainly he could be a man for some,
say winter one year, the next perhaps
some amalgam of spring and autumn.
The problem was that desire
had no season, was as present
when icicles dangled from the eaves
as when hydrangea blossomed
and something less than love
felt irresistible in elevators and back seats.
Just yesterday at the museum
he imagined one of de Kooning's
fierce women stepping out
of her painting to urge Vermeer girls
to reveal their secret angers,
give up their chaste bonnets,
and scream. He imagined Jackson
Pollock wanting to bathe with one
of *Les Demoiselles d'Avignon*.
That's how he walked the venerable
halls, his five senses wishing a sixth
as he went. And when he left, the streets
seemed full of desire, beyond all

equivalences, beyond anything that could be
fully controlled. Sometimes in the morning paper,
he'd read that the stars
and his birth month were happily aligned.
Sometimes they wouldn't be. Sometimes
there was nothing to do but declare
what he wanted, and live with the consequences.

Give me rain
lightning seems to be saying.
And a rogue cloud
(like a woman I know),
sensing some celestial command,
starts to resist
what appears so exclamatory.

And if a cloud could speak
I imagine it saying, *Crybaby, Crybaby,*
wishing in advance to shame
the darker clouds
and hold off the predicted deluge.

Everything is still now,
as if the universe has been
successfully chided,

as if one man's imagination
could alter the likely.

The day fades
then fades some more.
It appears dusk will have its day
and lightning will tire
of its poor percentage of success.

What's to be done
with shadowy men like me?
How to say to a certain woman,
Give me everything you have
and want her to hear
the smile in it, the furtive plea?

AT THE SCHOOL FOR THE DEAF

After three days of watching their slangy, fast-
    fingered exuberant talk,
then their slow, crude placement of words

on paper, I wanted only to reach the girl
    who'd do nothing
I asked. One morning she gave in,

wrote "Silence has a rough, crazy weather,"
    and shoved the paper at me,
this hearing person she didn't trust.

Oh I admired her resistance, and her
    great small truth about silence,
and she knew it, kicked the nearest chair

when I looked her way, turned her face
    into stone.
She must have known how soon I'd retreat

into my other, easier world. She must have
    known there'd be some cost
for compliance, and what she couldn't afford.

There've been others in my life smart enough
    not to let themselves
be loved by me, but I can't remember

wanting so hard what I couldn't get;
  one more line, I'd sign,
one more word. She wouldn't lift her hand.

Her classmates flashed fingers at her.
  She flashed back
expletives anyone could understand.

THE FAMOUS MAN

We knew he was dead
because the dead don't smile
unless someone works hard
with the lips, and someone had.
A profound local sadness
was everywhere felt. We
could hear several voices
praising the bold delicacy
of his work. No one said
his smile was really
a sardonic grin, or that
he was never as happy
as those lips would suggest.

I, for one, knew he was dead
because I felt suddenly free
of a standard no longer mine.
And of course he was dead
because he just lay there,
immobile, like a Calder without
a breath of air to move it.
In fact, he had become an *it*,
and those of us who knew him
noted how poorly
itness suited him, his pale demeanor
resembling nothing he'd been.

Real life, we agreed, was okay,
but we preferred this life now being made
of words, as he had, uncovering
what we didn't know was there.
We were his friends, and wanted
to throw light onto the ashes
before they became unstoried and urned,
loose sentiments strewn in a field.
But he was dead, goddammit, and now
it was about us. We'd toast
a few drinks to him back at the house.
He'd be in our thoughts until he no longer was.

THE ARCHITECT

loved the Möbius, and the sky's big suggestion
  of a universe, and now and then
would imagine a heaven as if it were his

to construct and manage, death just a pause
  before the real work would begin.
In truth, and in his practice, he preferred things

that had endings, was sure anything
  that goes on and on
was destined to mislead, be shapeless,

false. But still the idea appealed to him
  the way feelings appeal
to those who feel they should be thinking.

Some, the innocent, would call him the architect
  of infinity, which he wouldn't correct,
while the rest of us kept as quiet as we could.

When it comes to the underworld
and the fragility of guesswork,
what makes us think the dead
want evidence of our caring?
At the gravesite, a litany of roses,
good wishes and prayer.
And those who are pretending—
let's remember at such moments
everyone is an amateur of feelings.
Some of us will be the kind
who say nothing, pivot, and walk away.
Those who choose to speak
will discover it takes other words
to say the words they mean.

COME VISIT

On a day when all the news seems good, it must be
evidence of what I don't yet know. Surely some nation
or some someone must be seeking vengeance
at this very moment, or one of death's many special agents

has a plan with a reason behind it—god-voices once again
speaking demon language in his head.
Maybe for a while all the news is local, and therefore

a sweetness seems sustainable, but even then it might mean
that sociopath hasn't yet emerged from his basement,
is still the nice quiet man his neighbors, when interviewed,
will attest to. Kept himself to himself, they'll say.

I'm not trying to inform you, my friend, about what
you already know. Come visit. I need to talk to a betting man,
someone who still believes the future has a chance.

EVEN THE AWFUL

Ecstasy like awe hardly ever occurred,
though when it did it provided
its own definition. Still, I would prefer
an occasional bout of joy,
which I could recover from in a day
or so, and maybe even speak about,

whereas ecstasy (that one time)
made me silent, and awe was something
like Lazarus rising from the dead
and the populace uttering the equivalent
of "Holy shit," then falling
to their knees in bewilderment.

A nice day was nice, too,
as was a beautiful disappointment—
like fog obscuring a sunrise
I'd set my alarm to see.
I'd even settle for an evening
of small talk and inappropriate snorts

and guffaws with friends I was sure
were otherwise capable
of high-mindedness and hilarity.
Even an awful day now and then serves
to warn us what's out there, which doesn't
help, because here it comes anyway.

IF DARK CLOUDS

If dark clouds in the west suggest a storm
and one weather person says it will be a doozy
while another says it will pass just to your north
and has squiggly lines on a map to prove it,
and both broadcast from the same station,

who should you trust? Or is this mere showbiz,
a spectacle of disagreement among experts?
The woman weather person says, Even if he's
right, she'd prefer *a collision of fronts* to a word
like doozy, but smiles when she says it.

They both work for people who know weather
has become a business, thus her cleavage,
and his bowtie and casual mention of a doctorate.
Today, though, they agree it's serious business
if you live in Oklahoma City (you don't), or know

someone in the vicinity (you do), or if you live
elsewhere and have (this they don't say)
an imagination and a heart that can be broken,
or, more terrible, one that can't.
Their network knows we all have worries

beyond the vagaries of weather; its ads suggest
ways to lessen anxiety, and they recommend pills
that brighten your outlook if their side effects
don't kill you. And there you are in your living room
with the bemused worry of a groom whose bride
may actually show up this time.

The weather people are correct
in assuming you watch them for reasons
beyond discovering how to dress for the day
or if it's necessary to carry an umbrella.
The people you love, the few you can't bear,
are understandably not their concerns,
as they are sometimes not yours,

though today you're wishing one of the experts
would address the hidden relationship between
catastrophe and entertainment, and why there's
so much smiling. Now the weatherwoman points
with her pointer to a town not far away
from your town, a town that's in the path

(the psychopath she calls it—risking a weather joke)
of that funnel-shaped disturbance that will dip

randomly, she says, and have no respect
for churches or cattle or anything in its way.
Their producer must be pleased with how a tinge
of regret in her voice gels with her visible excitement.

You've always been the kind of man who wished
to be known for the quality of his yearnings,
regardless of outcome, but now you want
the storm that won't stop to stop, just stop,

and your friend who lives there in Johnsville
with his two bulldogs, Butch and Bella, you want
for all of them to be spared. You feel like
the Holden Caulfield of the Midwest.
Meanwhile, the sky has darkened to another shade
of black, and the wind, it . . . the weatherman says

it's time to make a statement. No, says
the weatherwoman, it's time for prophecy,
but he puts his hand over her mouth. These are
the asides they've learned that boost ratings,
some are even scripted, but statement or prophecy,

whatever it is this time, you see Johnsville
suddenly being tossed about, cars and houses
like out of control low-flying aircraft,
and your TV flutters, becomes snowy;
everything disappears from your screen.

It's a doozy for sure, though semantics
and right and wrong no longer seem to matter.
And now it's coming your way.
You retreat to the southwest corner of your cellar
with its little nest of candy bars and blankets.
The weather people, if you could hear them,

would be saying that's where to go,
and if the house comes off its foundation,
blows over your head, you'll live another day.
Your phone is ringing. Your phone still rings!
as something like the end of the world descends,

then manages to veer away, and you're alive,
your neighborhood still your neighborhood.
You wander outside with others risen
from their cellars, hugging in stupefied silence
everyone you pass, the only sound
the whirr of a copter overhead,
recording the scene for a future broadcast.

BE CAREFUL

Don't look an animal in the eye
if it's larger than you;
it will think you want to fight,

or believe you to be exceedingly careless,
a danger to your species.
There would be the spectacle

of your death to worry about,
a mauling caught
on camera, perhaps shown worldwide.

Which is why it's not worth it,
even if the eyes
are amber, flecked with gold.

The way you stare at beauty
means aggression
to, say, a tiger. Whereas people

who wear dark glasses at poker tables
love to be stared at.
They like to show how good they are

at concealment; to them your long stare
is a compliment.
But a tiger is made silent and therefore

dangerous by the same fixed look.
There's nothing more scary
than a big thing deprived of its roar.

Doesn't blood usually follow when language
fails? And you'd be wrong,
as some have been, to think an ape—

because he was once your brother—
would do nothing more
than stare back. Be especially careful

if he reminds you of one of those brothers,
long lost and unloved,
who suddenly appears out of nowhere.

I'm going to move your chair closer
to where the trapdoor is, so I'll be alert
to all the implications of your fall.
Of course I expect the usual resistance,
though as a character in my story
you'll not be given the strength to reach
the utility knife on the worktable,
and I, not you, will have the last word.

I want to breathe the musty basement air
(and witness your last breath) for the sake
of verisimilitude. I'll be in the act of inventing
the entire scene. As I begin to type,
you will not be happy at the way
I give you the desperate consciousness
of a dying man. But certain readers demand it.

Really, there's nothing you can do,
though it's important that you try.
In such a situation everyone tries.
A wooden coffin awaits you,
and the cemetery isn't far away.
I can only apologize that those pallbearers,
once your friends, will not be very sad

after it's all over. Your death will confirm
you were a minor character all along.
I wish you could understand that yours
was simply a life, childless, malleable,
that my imagination found itself needing.
Nothing personal was intended, or occurred.

THE FIRST PERSON

We admire those who, near the end,
bear pain with a certain public stoicism,
who remain interested in others
for as long as they can. The tacit bargain
we make with them is to be
as we've always been, their seriously
cheerful daughters, sons, or friends.

Then they hurt so much they prefer pills
to us, morphine to anything that smacks
of love. And when they shit their pants,
start to howl, we need to remember it's pain
that makes even the most selfless selfish,
they can't help themselves, and we must narrow
the distance—become an I or a me—

to involve the heart, let it into how we speak.
Because sometimes, my dear brother,
like you, the nearly dead never cease
to amaze. Between coughs you told
a bad joke, thanked us for enduring you,
made each of us feel, I was sure, like the first,
the only person, you wanted to reach.

III

AMBUSH AT FIVE O'CLOCK

We were at the hedge that separates our properties
when I asked our neighbors about their souls.
I said it with a smile, the way one asks such a thing.
They were somewhat like us, I thought, more
than middle-aged, less dull than most.
Yet they seemed to have no interest
in disputation, our favorite game,
or any of the great national pastimes
like gossip and stories of misfortunes
about people they disliked.

In spite of these differences, *kindred*
was a word we often felt and used.
The man was shy, though came to life
when he spotted an uncommon bird,
and the woman lively, sometimes even funny
about barometer readings and sudden dips
in pressure, the general state of things.
We liked their affection for each other
and for dogs. We went to their house;
they came to ours.

After I asked about their souls
they laughed and stumbled toward an answer,
then gave up, turned the question back
to me. And because mine always was
in jeopardy, I said it went to the movies
and hasn't been seen since. I said gobbledy

and I said gook. I found myself needing
to fool around, avoid, stay away from myself.

But my wife said her soul suffered from neglect,
that she herself was often neglectful
of important things, but so was I.
Then she started to cry. What's the matter, I asked.
What brought this on? She didn't answer.
I felt ambushed, publicly insensitive
about something, whatever it was.

It was a dusky five o'clock, that time
in between one thing and another.
Our neighbors began to retreat to their home,
but the woman returned
and without a word put her arms
around my wife as if a woman weeping
indicated something already understood
among women, that needn't be voiced.
They held each other, rocked back and forth,

and I thought *Jesus Christ*, am I guilty again
of one of those small errors
I've repeated until it became large?
What about me? I thought. What about
the sadness of being stupid?
Why doesn't her husband return
with maybe a beer and a knowing nod?

WHY WE NEED UNIONS

After Aesop

If the lion wants more
than his share, give it to him.
At least try, for Christ's sake,
to strike a deal.
Forget your zealous politics.

Don't be the ass, and want
to divide things equally
when equal you're not.
You'll be visited in broad daylight.
The jungle has its government.

The fox understands. After the lion
kills the ass for being an ass,
that is, for not knowing the limitations
of being clawless and without a plan,
the fox gives the lion a lion's share.

What's fair is for goose and gander,
for those capable of love, and even then,
even then . . . life being what it is
the rest of us spend most of it
dreaming of revenge.

All morning—because the mornings had been slipping
into afternoons with unnatural speed, leaving little to savor—
he promised himself he'd wake before even the hint of light.
When the sun rose, he'd say *Dawn*. And he'd name the first cloud
First Cloud, and this was how he'd try to begin it all again,
one ordinary event at a time, properly named. He'd prolong
breakfast with long pauses between bites and sips. He'd make calls
to friends who had drifted backwards into acquaintanceship.

MEN FALLING

It was another one of those mornings,
and she was thinking that if angels
really existed they would try to help,
perhaps slow things down
so she could make better choices,
remove the ifs and the downright no-goods
from the possibles.
                    Gray stones and gray pigeons,
and those men falling fast
from an ever-graying sky— why did
only the seemingly wrong ones hover
and tap on her window, ask as if they were
slumming to be let in? She was thinking
a woman needed an angel
    for every son of a bitch she'd ever known.
She'd seen her best friends disappear
into their marriages. Even when she spoke
on the phone to them, they weren't there.
How to live, what to do. she wrote
in her diary, omitting the question marks.
                    She was at the mercy
of whatever the wind blew in,
yet she had to admit some of the falling men
appeared decent, perhaps were on their way
to good jobs. But history instructed her
even the attractive ones were likely to return
at terrible speeds to their mothers,
desiring an attention she couldn't provide.

On the radio it was promised
that the grayness would continue,
and when the local weather gave way to news
of the world, citing prisoners on dog leashes,
a child born with twelve fingers— she sensed
the unreal slipping into the real, becoming it.
　　　Did she really want a man who'd fall
and land, and stay? And for how long?
Often in her dreams she'd conjure quiet men
with a gift for listening, but she'd wake
full of worry, fearing they were unable to hear
what she was unable to say.
　　　Many who continued their journey downward
were so beautiful in their descent
she wished she could wish for them a happy landing,
but she knew how hard the bottom was
and how lonely, and wanted for them
just some sad recognition—like her own—
of what they were missing.

THE MELANCHOLY OF THE NUDE

She was thinking it was time
to be naked again, to take something off
for someone more interested in her
than in art. She wanted to be treated
more by hand than by eye,

wanted her clothes pulled at, torn,
tossed on the floor. This sometimes
made it hard for her to pay the rent.
She was a professional nude, good
at being still for hours at a time,

and practiced at doing what she was told
in a world where she was both woman
and thing. Always she'd return from desire
to the equipoise of her job, sated,
almost penniless, and often with a smile,

which the artist—because the nude belonged
to him now—would try to ignore, or change.

THE OWNER OF THE BOUTIQUE AT REDWOOD FALLS

There came a time when she found pleasure
in saying the word *pussy*, alert to see whom it shocked
or didn't. It was the same time when *penis* often felt
like a mere gentleman of a word, though the thing itself
remained to her a sweet second best, an option. Pussy
was groove and tongue, sometimes a perfect fit,
which meant to her a connection
that didn't need to be explained.
It had a language unto itself, gospel-like, rapturous
oohs and throaty huzzahs coming from a church
in the woods with its doors always open.
She also liked saying *cock*, those early mornings
she heard it call to her from afar,
when she'd wake and begin to dream.
Finally, though, she had to admit a penis
was silly, mostly hiding, like a diphthong
in a sentence you had to work too hard to figure out.
Whereas pussy was something that could go
the extra mile, give repeat performances,
and was peculiarly hers. She knew how it worked,
and when it didn't want to, and what she wanted
to hear if she desired the naughty, the needed.

IMPEDIMENT

> *The loneliness thing is overdone.*
> —Edward Hopper, about responses
> to his work

Except for shoes
the young woman is naked,
in a chair, looking out
a fully opened window,
her face obscured
by dark brown hair.
Apartment? Hotel?
Outside, the obdurate gloom
of city buildings.

It's 11 A.M.,
Hopper's title says,
time for her to have dressed
a hundred times.
And it's the shoes which hint
of her desire to dress,
and of some great impediment.

Elbows on knees. Hands clasped.
The window she's leaning toward
is curtainless.
There's no sense she cares
she might be seen, or
that she wishes to show herself.

FOR SOME A MOUNTAIN

For some a mountain, say an Everest or a Kilimanjaro,
exists to be conquered, the kind of obvious big thing
my father, that valley dweller, would casually diminish.
What's wrong with life in the lowlands, he'd say,
why not just look up, enjoy imagining
how you'd feel at the top? And interesting people,
if you need them, are everywhere. They can be found
in a glade or a clearing, even in a suburb.

My father is dead; he only has the words I remember
and choose to give him.

If I were to say my need to define myself
involves breathing air not many have taken in,
and the excitement of a little danger, I'd hear him say
Do some good work, mow the lawn, carry wood
from the woodpile. Don't confuse the dangerous
with the heroic.

But the truth is I'd like to be a mountainizer,
someone who earns the pleasure of his reputation.
When it comes to women, I desire them married
to their own sense of accomplishment, each of us
going our own way, coming together when we can.

Not enough, he says. If they lack generosity
they take back what they give. If they have it
they remind you, ever so gently, that a man
who climbs mountains leaves behind his beloved.

It's impossible to win arguments with the dead.

Everywhere you go there's danger of being a no one,
my father insists. Is he changing his position,
or is that willful me changing it for my sake?
The grave was always his destination, the modesty
of his ambition obscured now by lichen and moss.
Comes the mountain before the reputation, I say.
Comes the unsure footing, the likely fall, he says.

ONE NIGHT AT MAMA SORRENTO'S

When a waiter brings my food
and says, "Be careful, the plate is very hot,"
I always touch it. I used to know why
back when why was important to me.
Maybe I thought such a minor act
of bravery would impress the person
sitting across the table. Maybe, if I
acquainted myself with the gradations
of heat, the varieties of fire, I could imagine
surviving longer the long journey to the grave.
I was pretty sure that the explanations, even if
I had one, would only lead to understanding,
which, like most therapy, makes us aware
of what we'll continue to do. One night
at Mama Sorrento's, our waiter asked
if everything was satisfactory? I wanted
to say, "No, how could that be possible?"
I didn't. But when he came back
a second time, wanting to know
if we needed anything else, I couldn't resist.

There was so much to worry about
and only a few heroes to right
all the wrongs, that soon we had
to invent superbeings that would
swoop down to recitify, out-joke
the jokers, keep the plutonium
hidden in a cluster of clouds.
Evil always has an advantage
and always succeeds
until its enormous feet understep
some moral chasm, or a damsel
held dear by the populace cries out
and is heard. Then we're made aware
evil's job is to galvanize the unlikely,
to stir the ordinary man.
Salvation, however, needs
more than one story, in more
than one language, its heroes perhaps
thinking something like how the hell
do I get out of this jam, something
like that, personal and small.

On gray forgetful mornings like this
sea turtles would gather in the shallow waters
of the Gulf to discuss issues of self-presentation
and related concerns like, If there were a God
would he have a hard shell and a retractable head,
and whether speed on land
was of any importance to a good swimmer.

They knew that tourists needed to placate
their children with catchy stories, and amuse
themselves with various cruelties
such as turning turtles over on their backs
and watching their legs wriggle.
So the turtles formed a committee to address

How to Live Among People Who Among
Other Atrocities Want to Turn You into Soup.

The committee was also charged with wondering
if God would mind a retelling of their lives,
one in which sea turtles
were responsible for all things
right-minded and progressive, and men
and women for poisoning the water.

The oldest sea turtle among them knew
that whoever was in control of the stories
controlled all the shoulds and should-nots.

But he wasn't interested in punishment,
only ways in which power could bring about
fairness and decency. And when he finished speaking
in the now memorable and ever deepening

waters of the Gulf, all the sea turtles
began to chant Only Fairness, Only Decency.

This time I came to the starting place
with my best running shoes, and pure speed
held back for the finish, came with only love
of the clock and the underfooting
and the other runners.
Each of us would be testing excellence
and endurance in the other,

though in the past I'd often veer off
to follow some feral distraction
down a side path, allowing myself
to pursue something odd or beautiful,
not trying to, but becoming acquainted
with a few of the many ways
to measure success and failure.

I had come to believe what's beautiful
had more to do with daring
to take yourself seriously, to stay
the course, whatever the course might be.
The person in front seemed ready to fade,
his long, graceful stride shortening

as I came up along his side. I was sure now
I'd at least exceed my best time.
But the man with the famous final kick
already had begun his move. *Beautiful*, I heard
a spectator say, as if something inevitable
about to come from nowhere was again on its way.

LET'S SAY

Let's say a regular evening's darkness
disturbs no one, as it shouldn't. Even
when a storm knocks down wires
there are phones that work in the dark

and cabinets with canned food
until help arrives. Occasionally we can turn
a bad day into an acceptable one
by drilling a cross-court backhand

past a bad-sport enemy, or getting to the heart
of someone's elusive heart. Still, there's no escaping
that you were born and haven't yet died.
For years suffering has been hanging around,

wanting its fair share of you. Let's say you've been
lucky so far. It's true that the moon is always shining
in one hemisphere or another, while the dark
deepens, settles, makes a home for the stars.

Let's say you think of it as your job to cast
a light on some of the empty spaces left by the gods.
What's a poet anyway but someone who gives
the unnamed a name? A see-er more than a seer,

a maker of what becomes obvious, that's been there
all along. What you unearth resembles,
you hope, the real. You want that boy
who used to read under the covers by flashlight

to once again be astonished.
Once again he is. Suddenly there's this country
of no longer hidden things, this other world
both of you are walking toward.

A SHORT HISTORY OF LONG AGO

Once it was possible to think I was happy
if I had food, shelter, maybe a companion or two.
I lived then without comparisons, mirrors, ambition.
Television was the Lone Ranger, Dragnet,
roller derby. I thought all bad guys would be killed
or elbowed out of contention. Wars were over,
and sex was whatever happened to others
after a kiss and before a jump cut to morning.

I lived in town, then a city, then on the edge
near the exit signs where the choices were.
Experience, meaning what I could learn
from failure, was just a decision away.
I wanted to move into a future, acquiring friends
as I spoke of James Joyce, Harold and Maude,
my blind, unsuccessful date with Liza Minnelli.
I read the Bhagavad Gita for pleasure, or so I said,

dared to speak of enlightenment to the enlightened.
I joked I would have tried to become a Navy Seal
if I hadn't known I'd fail the final test
of innocence and bravery. Couldn't any or all of it
seem true? I wanted to believe such a conjured life
could make me happy, but my memory is too good.
A bad memory is the key to happiness.
I apologize for everything I haven't done.